Mulberry

Mulberry

Dan Beachy-Quick

TUPELO PRESS

Acknowledgments

Among the many to whom I owe thanks for their friendship while, and guidance in, writing this book: Suzanne Buffam, Sally Keith, Tony Lacavaro, Srikanth Reddy, Donald Revell, Sergio Vucci, and Leila Wilson.

Many thanks, too, are due to the Lannan Foundation and The School of the Art Institute of Chicago for providing me with space and time to complete the manuscript.

My gratitude, too, to the editors of the following journals, who kindly placed *Mulberry* in their pages: *The Colorado Review, First Intensity, Free Verse, Interim, Word/For Word,* and *Slope.*

Mulberry
Copyright © 2006 Dan Beachy-Quick
ISBN-10: 1-932195-24-6
ISBN-13: 978-1-932195-24-8
Printed in Canada
All Rights reserved.

First paperback edition June 2006
Library of Congress Control Number: 2005911087

Tupelo Press
PO Box 539, Dorset, Vermont 05251
802.366.8185 • Fax 802.362.1883
editor@tupelopress.org • web www.tupelopress.org

Cover and text designed by William Kuch, WK Graphic Design

NATIONAL
ENDOWMENT
FOR THE ARTS

Supported in part by an award from the National Endowment for the Arts

Table of Contents

To the Reader   ix

•

"earthliness is my book multi"   /**1**

"Record no oiled tongue"   /**5**

"years in coil"   /**7**

"guess the house from the angle"   /**9**

"Posterity, this me is Now—"   /**13**

"that yellow silk not Chinese"   /**16**

"We'll walk toward the thought"   /**19**

"augury of in"   /**22**

"I said no prayers but had milk"   /**26**

"Each dumb alone, but"   /**28**

"the whorled is mazed"   /**30**

"east east the great lake"   /**32**

•

"record it here: veins dark and hot"   /**37**

"calm the sentence the lake will calm"   /**39**

"at the window when the wind blows"   /**43**

"without contraries is no"   /**47**

"dawns on this road so late tonight"   /**52**

"morning green through ivy"   /**55**

•

In Memorium:

Jean Sholiton Radam
Sol Radam
Bernard H. Quick
Barbara Palmer Quick

For Hana & Kristy—
in this in which the wild deer / startle, and stare out

For all are transparent, nothing dark or opaque,
each wholly revealed to each to its innermost
part; for light is transparent to light. For each holds
all things in himself, each sees all in every other,
so that all things are everywhere, all is all and each
is all, and the glory unbounded; for each of them
is mighty, even the small is mighty, and the sun
there is all stars, and each star the sun
and all stars.

—Plotinus

The bounded is loathed by its possessor.

—Blake

To The Reader

Years ago, while studying Chinese Art, and granted access to the innards of the museum, I found myself holding a pot over 6000 years old. It was as large as my chest, but astonishingly light—made to hold water, buried in a tomb. The potter rolled a lump of clay into a thin coil, and formed circle upon circle until the pot was done. Then he put his hand inside the mouth of the pot, and smoothed the coils into a solid wall—a wall that bore the indentations of his fingertips in which my fingers now rested.

The silkworm's cocoon—that result of the voracious devouring of the mulberry leaf, and so prevalent on my mind as I wrote the pages that form this book—is spun of a single thread. The worm spins a silken line in its mouth, and weaving its head back and forth, constructs around itself the dwelling from which the worm will emerge winged.

A quirk in my compositional habit is the unconscious substitution of the indefinite article *a* when I mean to write *I*. For instance, before correcting the above, I had written: *a found myself,* and *a wrote the pages.* Poetry does this work in us of making I anonymous. What is a poet? A person who says I for another. But I worried that I could not say I for myself.

I began to think, as many have thought, that the worm's work and the potter's work share the same nature. As I mulled my lines I thought the divergent strands of my poetic interests—early American history, Puritan diaries, language philosophy, art history, religious mysticism— were not divergent at all, but simply the weaving back and forth, as the head moves almost unnoticeably left to right and right to left as one reads, of those leaves I had devoured, those pages I read.

Of the pages to follow, it may be best to think of them as such a silken line, turning upon itself to create a home, for this *I* I am. Poetry riddles oneself with oneself by weaving one voice into many. It is no small hope to think these voices speak a poet's own life as they speak their own. Such is, in part, what a man meant when centuries ago he said: *I am myself the substance of my book.* Or what I mean now, in hoping that the one dwelling within the lines is the same one as he who wrote them— the same as he who much later will from them emerge.

•

Record no oiled tongue, diary—
Note my lantern bruises the low
Clouds with light the evening
We talked. Almonds in a bowl;
She ate none. I did
Not bid her remove her dark
Gloves as sometime before she had done.
Her dress not so clean as before.
A last brand not rescued to flame—
No billow but breath, and breath
Too short a line to twine
Our hands in marriage: I left
A last time. Her in widow's silk—
My lantern clothed in morning
Dawns on this road so late tonight
The white birches I believe,
I believe I could have loved
Her, her white wrists
White the birch trees by lantern bared,
Black gloves pulled off at night
Become the night . . . . Do you hear?
That pulse? The deer wander
Between her hands, glean fallen
Seed at hand, bed down in fallen
Needles and grass. Those green discs
Afloat in the night are their eyes
Caught in lantern light. Can it be
So many wake the forest glows
With sight? See and am seen. A pulse
At the stump is breath and rest
And breath again. Infinite
In store the game of this land.
Note the plumage of the turkey.
Note the thick meat at breast.

Sap: syrup. Pine: plank. A copse
Of wood is cord for furnace. A copse
Is cottage, too. The owl in the hollow
Tree screeches because I am too close
To truth. Note the almond
Tree overmuch with fruit. The almond
Pressed is oil sweet. The almond bit
Is a smoky meat that leaves—note it:
The tongue bathed in oil.

• •

years in coil
my hand in the mouth of him
who dug

clay
her lips final // his
fingers on her lips and mine

open her so

cheeks smoother inside her
mouth
a wall so ash
flame at tongue on tongue
won't

spill a
word or bone // the urn
your eye
closes

at night // no fingerprint
when cold we

entered sheets // the moon
a basement
of rubble in orbit

when my hand

to hold light
opened
the window
in the mouth of him

who smoothed the wall
of this urn 6000 years
in coil
my hand cupped // urn
in urn // your breast
no touch bares

bone beneath so ash
"I thought the moon was full
tonight"

my hand
in the mouth of burial
his wife
this urn I urn // my finger

his fingerprint so
held
I am his too
tired to say no

to not love what's not
mine

Eros, weaver of tales

wove coil in me // thumb
my thumb // your lips //
his
onlyiest my everywhere

spellbound in the un

guess the house from the angle
I held the rake
to rake the fallen acre of
leaves my father holds noon
over me is mine:

did not see the geese
southerly in   'v'
this year did not see
the southern door open to street
where she no longer
could walk I could walk
through horns on highway
to gather her white
envelopes between cars the geese

swift foot not sure
I ran the idle in my ear
the engine
from you to not hit
not hate nor hit you
the March sky that low
no furrow in shadow no water
not ice   wife, love
no cloud could cover that day
enough enough:

let the fierce cut stone sorrow

swallow the cellar each
step is stone and I step down
the geese in 'v' not seen
as grandmother dies in the south
bedroom curtains drawn weave light
I step toward that frozen

not ice the electric
plant in chainlink
pressed myself to the fence *Tres*
passers will be no cloud
could cover no cloud would
lie *to the fullest extent*
that day when earth took the wire's
hum on loan
my fury undone and me a distance
from you where I ran:

not to fuse the gray fuse
into my eye not a branch
to cocoon memory and me
the spark // filament // the thread-
source
inside:

slow down the leaf slow
noon is now
past the maple on the dying
grass I did not hold
her hand when her hand was
that leaf in the teeth
of the rake
swallowed another afternoon

I kissed her teeth through her
cheek
thin veil her skin draws back

the day // the same weave
I'm wearing that March
when I fury to remember fury
to remember myself as I was
that day I unraveled:

struck the *No Parking* sign so
not to strike you

that day again and must I
rewind my steps to sing

elm leaf a tongue tell truth
the acacia's thorns do not fall
thorns angle into
sky in cloud again and clear

lean west elm lean west
labor the leaf home
the rake points up when put down
the evening knows
the cellar will not glow
with that light I mean to give
you this vision reddening
bleeds but never
stains the cellar will in naked stone
furnish a tooth with meat
caterpillar undoes some leaf

my mouth // some leaf // into silk
we dress in leaves
then moths know to borrow
is to feed on light and flee if seen
in life a hole
in the sleeve of grandmother's blouse
she put on to greet a stain
of tobacco
remember when she couldn't not
breathe
and now
her lung a chart in a room

I will not sing

she can't eat meat she lives
on toast she spreads
her hand open when she breathes:

isolate fields all generate
horizon a thousand
furrows thread //
am I *of the law* unraveling
at a single point // you

the freezer humming beneath her
house // our hours

•

Posterity, this me is Now—
Record this Now. *Virginia, 1705*
Not always settled. I am settled
Over history's yellow pages, blank
Pages, must I write my old dark
Thoughts: Does time mask or unmask
Mind? This sweet almond now
In my mouth as in their mouths
Then, sweet in its rind, but silent
I think: I am blood at oak, my hand
A blood petal unfurled over oak,
My desk, my wooded den, a pistil,
A pen. Believe me: I speak honest
And true.

First.

Economy ravishing and jealous
In woods, the virgin woods.
Sap is sweet so sap quarrels
On the tongue. What is *worth*
Worth? Sap sweet so sap ambers;
In the virgin woods none can cut
The profit from the tongue. Amber
Gold so gold whispers at the edge
Of each, our minds. The Natives
Wear skins on skin; the women
Bare their breasts and do not
Blush. Was she a King's daughter?
She walked below the branches;
The sun thin in silken lines
The sated spiders left. Her brothers
Showed us what seeds to sow.
Glass beads contain light, a miracle

To trade. Her skin a syrup
Tone, the beads gold against her
Wrist glowed. Midnight her crown
Of hair plaited with one strand
Of gold, thin as day's edge when dusk
Both dulls and hones that glow.
"We'll barter it." Her brother feels
Cheated when we offer a bolt
Less of wool than he asks. Write it
Down. Profit in black ink. They close
Their eyes, quick as bark blinks
Down dark on axe's silver bite,
When the deal is done. The ledger's
Honest, "I am a liar. Be aware."

Then.

Pluck the withered gold at hand,
The pumpkin leaves yellow,
Sere and dust. Neglect the acre.
Let the green aphids multiply
And suck. We teethed our vision:
A yellow sort of isinglass dust,
Sunlit in silt, under the water
Of our stream. The squash blossom
Closed its eye; we squinted to see
Beneath the stream. That summer
We fed our hearts on dust. We grew
Dust in gardens. We grew rich
Until the gold sheen disclosed
It was but gilded dust. We lived
Some time on mussel, crab, berry,
Those fruits of the wild earth. No one
Spoke the word "starving." We were
Forced to be content with what fell
Just in our mouths.

Earlier Than First.

Thought in the forest speaks
A wooden chorus. My own voice
Multiplied the almond by the pine.
Roanoke, 1588. Repaired the houses
Now grown up with weeds.
We make wooden houses. How quiet
One voice, mumbling verses out
The wilderness, by the fire
In the corner. Bibles clothed in skin
As the Natives come clothed. *Exodus*
A comfort: to be chosen, safe,
God spoke in smoke by day, in light
By night. A manna faith—of manna.

When Mr. White arrived, late *August
1590,* he went to search for us. Found
Weeds grown among the wood
Homes. He found us removed
From this land. He heard us whisper.
He never heard from us again.
Notes we pinned to the trees told him
We moved to another
Island that forms the *sound*
(But we were not there).

We live in the *sound.* He found
Our voices pinned to the trees.

• •

that yellow silk not Chinese
the museum your throat
wound that day Kristy in shroud
no // in scarf, no // in veil

to see one painting: Tintoretto
Tarquin & Lucretia (1580/90)

courtesy broke the bed broke
the god knocked
to floor where the knife lay
she'd slay
herself later in shame at rape

I see I keep returning
here these months

sketch geometry to better sing
her left arm reaching up
completes him
violence his head forever
his right arm naked to her naked thigh
composition is need
forever is not choice
is not why I asked

you here head crooked in no
song do you see // pearls
her neck // the broken strand
3 pearls curve at curve of breast
in air // veil dropping to cover
her sex at sex
a pearl not shy in folds

will fall to calf the pearl at calf
will fall to floor and those

6 will roll out the frame
and us there now too

in time I meant to slow us
in air as pearls are slow

people walk through our vision
and don't look // their passing
a universe // each time
their teeth a world of pearl

not pearls I mean

a luminescence not time
gathers in the mouth

leaving through Chinese Art
the statues at death are royal company
the emperor's altar
people below the mountain buried
coiled around him he wove stone
into stone and each obeyed

and I mean Kristy to say
I'm one of those

I've thought I'm one of those
stones that slow

a soldier or no a juggler
with my hand
held out to catch the ball

that's never falling that won't
ever fall those pearls

continuous
that day I meant to be so still

and out
the door in December the sun
a light bulb caught in oak

the sun that March // months ago
your neck intersecting the whole
horizon a pearl at your throat
if you'd kiss me

if you'd kiss me again
I'd press noon to my thumb
and press thumb to your lip

to my tongue tip of pearl
tip of sun // Kristy
unwind your neck the yellow silk

• • •

We'll walk toward the thought
    of the lime-tree
Down the lane, the morning sun

In present tense, logic my lament
    in the nerve. A day
Drops down its night-edged skirt

Around the box-spring of our bed,
    morning past-tense,
When making love the larch needle

Green at window when wind blows
    etches—Do you
Hear?—an echo of pen on page

Writes a moan our murmur in ice
    on glass, light wakes—
This world that through desire is seen.

Months we ask ourselves to fold
    the clean sheets
Only to unfold again, those months

Folding our hands into our hands,
    asking the other
Do you see? No. Do you see?—

Now, again—green angle, sun-lit leaf
    on lime-tree
Down the lane behind your eye.

When I speak of you to you,
    when I collapse
Headache into a cup, my hand

On cheek, your cheek, cannot prove—
    touch never proves—
You a distance from me, the lime-tree

I see is not mine, behind your eye.
    All morning sun
Angled off the polished table

The blank page I suffered thought
    of you, if you
Can feel the headache in me

For me. I'll point at pain for you,
    eyes closed: an inch
And a half behind my left eye, here

If you could touch it, I could touch
    you. Dark logic, green hue—
The old days in me glow new,

The leaf-idea crystalline, and you
    in me, as if—
As if more than my idea's electric

Presence, a matter aches in my head.
    I will tell you
What causes pain. The sun so bright

Some mornings. All day the sun grows
    so bright shadows
Cry. I have heard you cry. I have

Cupped my hand to your cheek, comfort
    inside my head, the
Nerve crowds the world into the mind.

I miss you. Your shadow
    in the kitchen
Behind me. It's winter here

In me, and how can you?—how
    can you gleam so?—
Behind me, your lips asking

In shade, "Do you need an aspirin?"
    I think I do
See in your mouth's dark shadow

The lime-tree, dead all season,
    bloom again—first
The lime-tree in your mouth, leaf then light.

augury of in
scape of wood stress of wood
a pulse in sap // some heartwood
an artery a threadsource
in me and innocent
now this orbit in rings
of the tree in the yard of her
who passed

earth in the dry anger

now the dangerous song
occupies the middle thought

the furrowed thought the borrowed
thought the song unwinding
may be winged // as when

a child with her the woods of each
in danger not rain not lack
of the worm jaws and we
knocked cocoons into soapy water
to kill them and later I would
undo the silk to find pupa to find
wingstub but found only the weave
undone // the weaver gone

leaves // the broken green cup

noon over me was mine

the bitten leaf alarms light

my fingers joined are cracked cup
too and noon
is the caterpillar's // noon is the worm's
mouth a

verse a writer at the turn
an eagle talon a nib a feather a nib
at margins
above the white field each noon
the white field blusters *blous*
the cut worm forgives

plow the source is unknown
not fear engraved

pen the cursive
line forgives the plow

blousteropherous humbles
my eye at the edge
of the line a long time that gypsy
moth the mind
reads backwards the same line
so the field is plowed west-east
then east-west
the page is the reverse of day
and the page is day doubled

a worm inched up the tree we circled
an adhesive metal so thick
in number the worms all summer
crept upon those caught and dying
and so themselves fixed on metal
shining mar on death
crept upon those caught and dying
the dark bridge across the metal band
the bridge alive and those crossing

to gain the green leaf // height of

eagle at the root
borrowed from Old English *egle*
from Old Provencal *aigla*
from Latin *aquila* originally black
eagle feminine of *aquilas*
dark-colored the color of storm cloud
probably from *aqua*

water at the root of the bird

the eagle born of flood
maintains every mountain its nest
in drought
the eagle I think a silver coin
I think a thirst no a feast

my eye humble in the plow
reads the dust
that road clings to cloud
half this road is cloud and white
the field an unpaved dark

storm rises in sheets from sheets
blank with horizon how to read
west from the edge where red sun sets
the red sun sets on *"a...*

long time ago" I thought the gypsy

moth destroyed the trees not me

unwinds the tree along the crease
of age its rings
in one long line each year sings
the heartwood in time
to the worm's jaws the eagle's wings
my pulse in flight
a lullaby at the wrist
all begins arterial and the artery ends
my heart in the gypsy's jaw
the eagle's talon plows the field
but does not end the drought
the broken leaf lets noon through
into my hand // born of water // wood floats
in time the eagle will melt back to warm
water the worm will question
with its body the whole moth it made
time a silk ribbon unwind the tree
in me // the threadsource // my mouth
thirsty but no eagle famished but no

worm
do you see it o noon
there in the hole in the leaf is
the whole day

•

I said no prayers, but had milk
For breakfast. A white page
Bound between black covers—
That secret page is thick cream
Before confession curdles the blank
Day dark with ink. Such eclipse
At noon will outlive noon; does;
Undays the heart and heat of day.
I record it here. Veins dark and hot.
My heart in bright eclipse, filled
With ink my red lips blush more
Red at word unsaid, words I will
Not say, but—darkly—I must write.
I said no prayers, but...I rose
Early. The rose open before the day;
Found beetle in rose; "let it feast"
I thought; let it stay. *I danced*
My dance. The White Plum in blossom
Walks its scent through the willing
Air—I breathed in the whole bride
Whose white bud will purple later
Into plum; I'll bite. I do. I often bite.
The White-Throat in the flowering
Bush flits and sings; I see it
With my ears. *I danced my dance.*
My wife's white throat in bloom
Above her purple dress. She cast
Her eyes sky-ward when she saw
The look in my eye this afternoon.
"Did you practice your Hebrew?"
She asked. "I spoke a page." The blank
Day bound between black covers:
Night gone and night so soon to be.
The White-Throat flew out the bush

When I neared; a blossom knocked
From stem by flight. I picked it up.
An inchworm on silk angled on breeze
That through the plum tree breathed.
I let the green inch alone to eat my leaf.
I walked in the garden till ten
And then committed uncleanness.
I said my prayers.

Each dumb alone, but
   when the lone violin doubles
there are notes we hear
   only sung against the other's song;
then we are not deaf.
   I hear the song approaching
scherzo in my own mouth,
   now when you're near me,
these broken days in me,
   my words, I hear them speak to me
in your mouth. The world
   near in pain, clearer in pain.
I saw a pigeon's wings pinned
   at breast but the pigeon gone.
I found some nameless thumb
   dark in the sky she wanted
a photo to remember: the picture
   under the thorn bush thrown—
discarded square of self-marred sky
   half-buried in moss and mud so blue.
On the bus to work I saw
   a scrap fluttering behind metal
grating of the heater's fan
   become the somber, filthy moth
whose sullen, patient, caged flight counseled
   divorce all hope from ends—
won't console, love won't console
   love is light angled
against light to see. The baby reaching
   his left hand to his mother's face—
she nears, says, "Here I am." His right
   hand against light in the window…
the lake edge near, so near today,
   I'd never noticed…hadn't known…

opposite me, the girl, her eyes
    the same gray as the gray water—
how strange she is in her body,
    looking at me and not at me, the lake
encircling and spread out behind her
    face, a veil parted when mourning
is done. The violin string
    of one strand of silken hair sings
the taut line at horizon
    of the lake that will not end.
The lake edge's whorl in finger
    print of thumb, the whole lake
in the baby's mouth, the window
    so bright, his mother's face full
with cloud, the thumb's song
    dark on moth's paper wing,
the girl's eyes are pigeon's wings,
    and now I hear the violent now
aria around me:
    what endures by not enduring:
the gray lake's lungs, body,
    feathers into waves
at a child's breath, the missing
    body to the bird's gray bone,
the lake is the pigeon's breast,
    wings in the baby's mouth breathe,
the thumb in cloud
    plucks the truant string—
whose song descends blue from cloud
    and lowering says, "Here I am."

• • •

the whorled was mazed
pine siskin on pine cone
child at lake edge
flat water float stone

my heart what arrow struck
struck feather first
whole horizon sharp or just
the blade edge last

world and thumb in echo
in orbit in inkpot
how long harmony worlds us
in us warbles a nerve

a song in migration
warbler mouths the whorled
tree less empty the sun
ends on the lip (of no nest

earth) in me loam on loan
my ear small in it
my eye small in it
lake deafens when lake knows

hadn't you bit hadn't you tongue
nerve wobbles if star is spun
is spanned a child in orbit
of lake edge empties his hands

lash bone to lonely blood
some deaf thumb inks
the star in dust and ashes we
swallow nuthatch whitebreast and gull

think gall spare vowel a
child skips stone after stone
water warbles lake lake calms earth
earth borrows him and earth knows

*

the world was made for my sake

*

*

I am but dust and bone

*

east east the great lake
wakes my song in no ear
melody so folded in blood
to sing might unvein me

warblers sing east they know to stop
at lake edge in the pinion in the reed
hear a yellow song in juniper
the needle in their blood composes

their song in my hand
if I pray

my wife in wood how many flowers
stalled in wood

blessing rooted in blood blood is
rooted in blossom

my grandmother in ash

water thin veil thin silk

threads ripple out the wings
the dying bee's song
beaten into water only the eye
at lake edge can hear the tune

I hear the tune I see I do
hear sweet honey sweet sap
here is the sun // the sun in cocoon
in cloud at night

a sentence in love

the old moon in the arms
of the new

moon and my arms
pulling the silk out my mouth

swaddling cloth prefigures the shroud
the threadsource inside me now
that thread taut in spider's web
is silken in the silkworm's mouth
the panicked bee must tune its hum
when honey is caught is harmony
I sing my love to thought
In time // a silken art // philosophy
in margins // the eye cocoons
within the tongue one silken strand
I wind my patience into ecstasy I chew
silk to sing my dark heart again

blood in ribbons glows through skin
my hand held to flame
reveals the moth wing in the vein
my hand the lamp

my own blood flutters to and seeks
the moth wing in the vein

⇌

my vein in the moth wing
blood flutters blood seeks
the moon within a hand
my hand veined to veined wing
my hand apart from flame
skin woven bright // bright veins unlaced

again in my heart some dark silk
sings patience into ecstasy
the tongue unwinds
that silken margin the white eye
not in thought not philosophy
my love in song not time
honey is gold gathered into harmony
the harp strung in the bee's wing
is silken in the silkworm's mouth
the spider attends the taut
threadsource inside me now
the shroud predicts the swaddling cloth

pulled out my mouth my
arms the moon

new cusp of
light limns the old edge we

love in sentences

the grammar in the cloud
undone by light the sun
sweet in honey sweetens sap
in my ear I hear

echo back the song concentric
in circles the lake will deafen
its edge will sing back each thread
beaten from wings
the dying bee will leap up

smooth lake the bridal veil

ash in water is ink

blossomroot bloodblossom sharp
blessing in blood

not in knot not in burl a flower
wife of wooden petals

make my hand of song

my finger a needle of blood
let me point to yellow
song bright among reeds the pivot
at lake edge none sleep warblers
sing east and grammar me east

so song rising unveins me
blood so folded in harmony
my ear wakes in song
the great lake // east east

. . . .

I record it here: veins dark and hot

with cloud, the thumb's song

in orbit, in inkpot

lash bone to lonely bone

sing each against the other's song

as pine siskin sings to pine cone

thrown under the thorn bush

the heart and heat of day

these days broken in me,

these words, I hear them speak to me

my ear small in it

then I am not deaf

I hear the song approaching:

The White-Throat flew out the bush

and feathers became those waves

of the lake that will not end

flat water float stone

earth borrows her and earth knows

                                        a song in migration

whose white bud will purple later

not night gone but night so soon will be

a beetle in a rose let feast

                              I'd never noticed // I hadn't known

my wife's white throat in bloom

                              in her mouth the world

red at words unsaid, words

                              near in pain, clearer in pain

                              love

                              won't console, love won't

bind between black covers

some

                              deaf ear fluent in celestial spheres

confess the blank

day is dark with ink

                              when she nears, saying, "Here I am"

                              looking at me and not at me

her eyes sky-ward when she sees

calm the sentence the lake
will calm // breath at pivot
breath gathers itself in a comma
a comma informs the wave

weave new panic into water
so calm will curl the new
dead leaf red as dusk
settling this sun
drowned lonely in the crest

of cardinal I cannot quite
catch nor quiet
mars in rust my breath in rose
breasted grosbeak flees
the wound it wears I wear
the calm lake winged into scarlet wave

the panting wave

panten to breathe hard and quickly
borrowed perhaps shortened
from *pantaisier*
oppressed with nightmare struggle
for breath during nightmare
from *phantasioûn* to form
images subject to hallucination

nightmare tangent to reeds
why wind in me

sings my lung the lake
surface in unblessed rage
not for order   scavenging
lullaby   the gullswings
darken at tips into crows
my rage and one reed
sings *Childe* and I reply *My Lord*

it sang   *awemore awemore*

gulls in water madden memory
into mist the furious
lake in certain light stands
up and is the sky

a cocoon of unknown origin
oak gall or berry
seed or shell
of mussel or of clam not
nest the shell of an egg
a word on loan

woven in cloud to dim
swell or darken
burst the not
sun nor rain the crow

called open my
grandmother's hand her palm
the bed of the whole
lake she breathed

"Danny" a needle spinning north
in one eye // the whole lake
in her palm // the waves
she unfolded into shroud
and put the dark lake on

my wife shoulders my madness

nights I wake screaming

her hand a comma curled inside
me calm // calm

calme from *calma* from *kaûma*
the heat of day
time for rest   stillness from
kaíein to burn

the red-winged blackbirds calm
at noon in reeds weave flame

weave in the sunlit pattern
or plunged in shadow the days
each with the scarlet

thread through the whole warp
and wave of the design
time almost disappearing in its dark
cocoon then bright
silk emerging at the full inspiration

woke with the worm in my mouth
raving
gulls panic the god contagious
fear in water
the cloud denies my eye
formed dust into delight

my wife in lake her hand
opening into ripple   love
I won't remember I won't
wrist my wish
back to her body her pulse
quicker than lake records
with wave her heart gathering
in panic // those gulls // her pulse
panting wings her lips
parting from water and what
water imagined water was
for me // sky cloud love // wife
who in pain who in panic
the gullswings struck her hand
in water to rise from water
her hand by touching
her hand with flight died

the whole vibration repeating
the scarlet lake at dusk
shimmers furious before it calms
and cloaks soft that breath
my breath exhaled the framework
in delay I fill my lungs
again I see the indestructible
work of breath is breath
not to be lost sight of again

• • • •

at the window when the wind blows

the green angle again

on my tongue

these months

a luminescence not time

and us here now too

our voices pinned to trees

now grown up with weeds

of each, our minds   the Natives

gather in the mouth

to record one violent passion

in my mouth as in yours

the wilderness

laments the nerve

of pen on page

recording this Now

not settled

in my head

a universe each time

      the sun becomes so bright

each day I meant to be so

sunlit and

just in our mouths

the sun thin in silken lines

      your neck the broken strand

            in present-tense

            pain an inch

      down the lane, behind your eye

            the morning sun

gold so gold whispers

      now ever as now

on the tongue

      if you'd kiss me

            your lips asking

      ourselves to unfold

in wooden chorus my own voice

the virgin woods none can cut

                   a door in the sun

                   we look through each morning

                   walking toward that thought

                   in shade

         forever

this island that forms our vision

                   Now

                   I'll tell you what causes pain

both dull and glowing

                   all day

                   the world in the brain

                   folding months

into pages, must I write my old dark

                   shadows that cry

by night a faith

if you'd kiss me

I'd keep returning here

for you, if you

unfurl in oak

for me, I'll point you at

noon

when last year blooms again

slow in air

that gold sheen discloses

eyes closed

in me, as if, as if more than

sound we live in

thought the forest speaks

morning, the blank

star and each obeyed

this sweet almond now

unsettled

and true

without contraries is no

moth born with eyes of what
devours it on wing and will

progress my heart

haunted leaves in caterpillar's
mouth is my mouth
gift and green and
grist again blossoms trans
lucent silk to pure extent

inhabit   grand   massacre
mother   acres
of oaks gifted to blight

in wings her house who died

barnswallows dive murderous
down I dive in dust
I did not want nor threaten

mudnest woven with dead
grasses me
woven with dead

memory to cut hope
into nest
the lawn always in need
she must watch and did
at window
the sere august end at ends

that destruction be precise
I disappear into my gazing
at oak my eye
seized in light leaves live by

green eye the sun

"Son"   a greening star

worm's mouthful of star
a lifetime in the jaw so mute
so mute our galaxy's merest
heat   instant   light in leaf
digested becomes the never fed
hunger of moth for moon

so love hungers me back
whose blood in me billows
to nebulae in you   your hand
in the redshift a dove no
a devotion

heartsource repeat this song
with patience pluming past
patience not to peace not to
coo
lullaby that sun
infant in the pyresmoke
of that star whose failing

light collapsed in light

dust to grace another's glow

spiral   galaxy
thumb   print   whorl

barnswallow's secret is

grass in celestial weave
sewn whorl
in mud those swallows
nest whose life once disclosed
never touches earth
again // I found the small
eggs broken in garage
the yellow yolk in dust
feathered and stellar plumed

stark angel touched by time

she pointed me fireflies // stars
winged below stars
not-winged // all June
I am audience to actual
cosmos blinking night
the universe seen is the same
universe lived // there is no periphery //
shifting blue to near
the center // my eye // the grave attention
in the black hole that light
cannot escape from
I did trespass to see if true

what she said of fire

alone in my room that night
no light save the moon's
pale grid on window screen
my breath inhaled stellar and
exhaled luna
moth wide as my hand never
caught I took the firefly
cupped in my hand and ex
tinguished with my thumb
its life upon the wall and
it glowed // in time

it dulled but I saw
the fading green pivot of morning
prescient on my wall

now in me glowing

owl's call bright in woods

no trespassing there is none

I am less	angry
less of anger	now
now I inherit	dawn

• • • •

dawns on this road so late tonight

that pulse // the deer wander

                                        spellbound in the un

                                                  opened

                                        fingers on her lips and

                                              when my hand

                                                  closes

those green discs

afloat in the night are their eyes

becoming night // do you hear

                                              that digging

                                        in the mouth of burial

her white wrists

are wood for furnace

and breath again // infinite

                                        I thought the moon was full

                                        in the mouth of

                                        this urn I urn

                                        to hold light

                                        in coils

between her hands // glean

                                        a wall so ash

our hands in marriage

                                        my hand cupped in urn

is cottage, too // the owl in hollow

                                        bone below so ash

                                        my thumb your lips

                                        won't

                                        not love what's not

clothed in morning

                                        flame

                                        her lips final // mine

caught in lantern light // can it be

I believe I could love

                                        word and bone and urn

                                                open her so

with light // a pulse

wakes the forest and the forest glows

because I am too

                                            tired to say no

                                                don't

                                        window my wife

                                                don't

                                            open her so

morning green through ivy
leaves resuscitated
on window let us also breathe
our own breath and

the birds their blood in arrows
settle into nest from migration
the cloud of their song woke
me // stormed in me // a waterfall
in the thrush's call // a star flick
ering in the sparrows

we are not the woods if we
whisper the woods
quietly to ourselves we
witness our hands
walking into the forest we are
two rooms who think

alone // unless

my ear saw the cardinal my eye
heard the scarlet
tanager I could not
show it to you yesterday
it existed as I exist
now to you or the water pipit
bobbing at burble of creek to one
musical strand it heard and was
harmony of and I

saw from my distance

the web we step through to enter
woods:

spider sews one point to branch
and leaps where wind carries
sews one point of silk to fern
and leaps to where wind carries
until the web in logic

sees the plank in pine
do you see the house already built
the oak desk I think at the dark
cherry night
stand for your closed book
by the bed we keep a light to turn off
do you hear our whole house
swaying in the wind those birds
are not crying out in fear
those birds are singing nuptials
outside our house already built
in the green canopy the quoin of air

illumined always as it illumines
let us be truer
fact asleep below love a-leap // no
cornerstone no
cement save song do you
hear above us the river strong
in leaves the rubble
wind flows over and is not wind

river the rubblesource the river
ripples over to sing

us and the silken nest
weighs the beech branch down
in horror the multi
tude breathing in a single
lung and one

cocoon countless in turns
the transparent ever
winging itself past hunger
glows as we
glow is woven of one single
thread and no

love thinks separate
the weaver from the wing

I say now I love you
with the worm in my mouth
spinning my words
into your ear and your listening
volumes pupa
in the elm's crotch and oak knot
do you hear as I hear
the old sins blossom from diaries
and become the faith leaves
live upon we eat not ink
but the light that burns in the blank
page so ink can more unselfish sing

so the wounded deer leaps highest

so heart quickens

my hand cocooned in your hand
to become each one
half a wing of luna
moth waiting in woods for night's
blossom the moon

in borrowed light

through dark unfathomed the dead
star's light still lights on leaf a
finite edge we
loathe the bounded and nowhere

witness a cosmos in fetters

the woods lit by the lantern
blown out our eyes
by bright stars no longer

thinking love is bright

our woods and us
some star's thought so the wild

iris angles up in sun
so sun is all
stars and us the worm
whose hunger sated in leaf again
becomes hunger insatiable

not for fact // this world in which

nothing in the eye the instant dead
stars cast out countless shrouds

morning's bright pall // Venus ascends

ceaseless and wary

the weak light one upon the other throws

each moon waxing to each moon
of the other's face in full

caught
not in gazing
at light

we are what light gazes on

lumen ensouling love

so sigh so spiders feast by night
so whippoorwills cry "poor
will" so bobolinks wear the morning
sun behind their heads unseen
so light divides in two the star
light sprang from and sews together
again that star in us your sweet moan
moon your linger languor your
tongue on your lips not to speak so
the moon glows on your lips in me
the jack in pulpit blooms by night
so I bloom so I give me to you
so the appletree in flower proves
not fruit but the sun

in the mouth of the worm
who grammars these woods
into this world whose song is

Notes

"Record no oiled tongue" takes as its source and inspiration Samuel Sewall's *The Diary of Samuel Sewall, 1642-1729.*

"Posterity, this me is Now" takes liberty in retelling Chapter 1 of Robert Beverley's *1705.*

"We'll walk toward the thought" owes a debt to Gottleib Frege's essay "The Thought."

"augury of in" and "without contraries is no" owe their openings to William Blake.

"I said no prayers, but had milk" takes as its source and inspiration William Byrd II's *The Secret Diary of William Byrd of Westover,* 1719-1720.

The two lines ending "the whorled was mazed" are taken from Thomas Traherne's *Centuries of Meditation.*

The final stanza of "calm the sentence the lake will calm" owes a debt to John Ashbery's *Three Poems.*

Throughout *Mulberry* lines touch upon Blake, Dickinson, Herbert, Hopkins, Oppen, Stevens, & Simone Weil.